Little Mercy's
First Murder

Little Mercy's First Murder
a musical

Book & Lyrics by

Morwyn Brebner

Music by

Jay Turvey & Paul Sportelli

Little Mercy's First Murder
first published 2003 by
Scirocco Drama
An imprint of J. Gordon Shillingford Publishing Inc.

Music by Jay Turvey and Paul Sportelli

Scirocco Drama Editor: Glenda MacFarlane
Cover design by Terry Gallagher/Doowah Design Inc.
Cover photo (from left to right) of Jeff Lillico, Neil Barclay and Jane Johanson
is by Cylla Von Tiedemann
Author photo by Cylla Von Tiedemann
Printed and bound in Canada

We acknowledge the financial support of The Canada Council for the Arts
and the Manitoba Arts Council for our publishing program.

Canadian Cataloguing in Publication Data

Brebner, Morwyn
Little Mercy's first murder/Morwyn Brebner.
A play.
ISBN 0-920486-47-9

I. Title.
PS8553.R3734L58 2003 C812'.6 C2003-903948-X

J. Gordon Shillingford Publishing
P.O. Box 86, RPO Corydon Avenue, Winnipeg, MB Canada R3M 3S3

for Urjo Kareda

Morwyn Brebner

Morwyn Brebner's first play, *Music for Contortionist*, premiered at the Tarragon Theatre in 2000 and was published by Scirocco Drama in 2001. Subsequent plays include *Liquor Guns Karate* and the short farce, *Matador Love*. Morwyn lives in Toronto, where she is a playwright-in-residence at the Tarragon Theatre. She is a graduate of the National Theatre School. Her most recent play is *The Optimists*.

Characters

MERCY

WEEGEE

COP

SAMMY .... doubles with OLD MAN

NORMA ....doubles with WITNESS

MATRON .... doubles with PAPERBOY

WITNESS .... doubles with NORMA

INFORMANT ... doubles with MATRON and PAPERBOY

PAPERBOY

Setting

The action takes place in various locations in an imagined 1942 *film noir* Manhattan.

Production Information

Little Mercy's First Murder was first produced as a co-production between Tarragon Theatre and Shaw Festival and premiered at the Tarragon Theatre, Toronto, on January 14, 2003, with the following cast:

WEEGEE .... Peter Millard
MERCY .... Melody Johnson
COP .... Neil Barclay
SAMMY, OLD MAN, and others ...... Tony Nappo
MATRON, INFORMANT, PAPERBOY
and others .... Jane Johanson
NORMA, WITNESS, and others .... Jeff Lillico

Directed by Eda Holmes
Music by Jay Turvey and Paul Sportelli
Musical direction by Paul Sportelli
Set and Costume design by John Thompson
Lighting design by Andrea Lundy
Choreography by Eda Holmes and Jane Johanson
Stage Manager: Alison Peddie

A staged reading of *Little Mercy's First Murder* was first presented as part of Nightwood Theatre's Groundswell in June, 2001.

Overture

Scene 1

Lights up. Early 1940s New York, tiny tenement room. Twin bed, hot plate. Huge short-wave radio dominates the head of the bed, hissing. WEEGEE enters. He chews an unlit cigar end. He wears a rumpled trench coat and greasy suit. He has a permanent five o'clock shadow. At first he seems exhausted; actually, he has so much energy he rarely needs to sleep. He carries a Speed Graphic camera with a huge flash. He thunks it down onto the floor, sits on the bed. He sighs deeply. He looks to the audience.

WEEGEE: I think I'm an egomaniac.

He unfurls a huge yellow-stained handkerchief.

Everything I see, I think I made it up.

He blows his nose hard, then reams it out with the cloth.

Lights up, tiny tenement room. LITTLE MERCY sits on the edge of a fold-out couch. She's tiny, early thirties, housedress, man's cardigan. Her hands are clasped in her lap, her shoulders hunched with worry. A large bulk lies under the blanket beside her. A knife handle sticks out of the blanket. A phone on a long cord sits on her lap.

MERCY pokes the bulk beside her. Nothing. She picks up the phone.

MERCY: Hello, police? I'd like to report a death.

WEEGEE's radio begins to go off—copspeak, "ten-eleven at little West 12th Street..." WEEGEE grabs his camera.

Black.

Scene 2

A FLASH. A COP stands with MERCY above the sofa bed. WEEGEE skulks around the room, taking pictures. He shoots with the viewfinder at his chest, not looking through the viewfinder. The COP peeks under the blanket at the body. It smells.

COP: Phew. Well well well well.

MERCY: You want some coffee?

COP: Don't make coffee.

MERCY: No?

COP: No.

He takes out a pencil.

COP: Let's start at the beginning. Your name?

MERCY: Mercy Callaghan.

COP: Victim's name?

MERCY: Mercy Callaghan.

COP: *(Very dry.)* So it's a suicide?

MERCY: Oh no please don't...!

She looks away as the COP pulls the knife from the body. It's surprisingly long.

COP: What was this for? Gutting elephants?

The COP puts the knife in a paper bag, writes "KNIFE" on the bag. WEEGEE snaps a picture.

WEEGEE: I saw a man tonight, fall out a window, four stories up, land on his feet, and keep running.

COP: Oh yeah? Was he being chased?

WEEGEE: I have no idea. You would have thought his legs were made of metal. He fell, he landed, he ran. Incredible. Miss, why don't you stand a little farther from the body.

She doesn't. WEEGEE continues, to the COP.

The best thing was, his ladyfriend was watching, from above, from a window, you gotta understand, and I couldn't tell if she was more dejected when he fell, or when he got back up! Miss...move to your left.

COP: Just half an hour ago I pinched a shoplifter had an entire fur coat stuffed down his pants.

WEEGEE: That's quite a magic trick.

COP: It's nothing compared to where he hid the rack of ties he stole. Your guy get caught?

WEEGEE: Well this is the funny thing. By the time I get there the guy's been shot. Miss? To your left.

MERCY: I will not.

The COP snorts out a laugh.

WEEGEE: "You will not"?

MERCY: And I find your stories extremely unlikely. Especially yours. Men don't fall out fourth floor windows and keep running. They just don't.

WEEGEE regards her, licking the corner of his mouth.

WEEGEE: What, are we starved for imagination here?

MERCY: I think you'd find I'm anything but.

WEEGEE: I wasn't paying attention. Who is she? Did she find the body?

COP: She made the body. Meet Mercy Callaghan. As far as I can tell she murdered her mother, other Mercy Callaghan.

WEEGEE: Is that so. I suddenly find you infinitely more interesting, Miss. Stand in the center there why don't you.

MERCY: I didn't kill her! I didn't! She was dead already. I stabbed her—!

COP: You stabbed your dead mother?

MERCY: Is it a crime?

COP: Uhn...?

Nobody knows. MERCY steps up.

Proust says a madeleine reminds you of all things
I've never had a madeleine
Freud says that every man anticipates his father's
death
What about a woman then?
A woman with no madeleine?

I wouldn't eat a cookie to remind me of my life
I'd rather eat that knife
A hundred knives and razor blades would taste to
me like lemonade
But the taste of my past
That's like drinking piss from a glass.

Little Mercy Callaghan, born in a filthy tenement
room
In nineteen-ten at the stroke of noon

No midwife to yank me from the womb
But the neighbourhood whore from the neighbouring
room
My mother was too drunk to push

Little Mercy Callaghan, eight years old with a rattling
can
Begging for pennies from a dressed-up man
"For a bowl of soup or an end of ham, sir?"
Living on scraps too little for a hamster
The money went to mama's "medicine"

Little Mercy Callaghan, fourteen in a dress for a bigger
girl
Leaving school to make her way in the bigger world
Gets a job at the library cleaning the floors
Books like jewels against dark marble walls
So nice, so nice to read and mop

Then Big Mercy Callaghan, dead drunk opening a can
of beans
Dropped the lid then passed out on the sharp thing
She awoke in the ward with the DTs, twitching
And missing one leg below her right knee, gangrene
She said, "Now who will look after me?"

I will
I will
I will
"I will."

Proust says a madeleine reminds you of all things
I've never had a madeleine
Freud says that every man anticipates his father's death
What about a woman then?
A woman with no madeleine?
Like Little Mercy Callaghan.

WEEGEE takes MERCY's photo.

Do you know what's incredible?

MERCY: I don't know.

COP: Every crime is mitigated. Every single one: I was drunk, officer. He hit me first. I didn't mean it. I slipped. Sure. You wouldn't be human, Little Mercy Callaghan, if you didn't feel you were misunderstood. But let me tell you something: When two people argue, let's say, a situation can be relatively equal. Mitigating factors on both sides. But as soon as one of those people becomes dead, things change. Death's an irrevocable act. Not subject to mitigation. Do you see my point?

MERCY: I—

COP: Do you see my point? Things have changed. Irrevocably. Now sit. The coroner's going to arrive. He's going to expertly pronounce your mother. You'll be arrested, you'll be tried, and then…who knows. *(To WEEGEE.)* You wanna play cards?

WEEGEE: Nah. What happened to your partner?

COP: They decided I don't need one. I'm that efficient. *(To MERCY.)* And by "who knows" I mean:

He makes a quick hanging gesture.

WEEGEE: Ah, they don't hang people any more.

COP: No, they use the electric chair. But I'm not that good of a mime.

He lays out a deck, begins to play solitaire.

WEEGEE: Spell your last name for me.

MERCY: Gee-oh-tee-oh-haich-ee-double-L.

WEEGEE: That'll look cute in the paper.

MERCY: You're a reporter?

WEEGEE: I'm a photographer. Weegee the Famous.

MERCY: That sounds wishful.

WEEGEE: Occupation?

MERCY: Movie star.

WEEGEE: All right, Miss Go To Hell, maybe you could take a second between scripts and give me a quote for my photo caption. Don't worry—I'm an advocate for the downtrodden. I'll write something nice.

MERCY: Then write that someone should send me a hundred dollars so people like you stop calling me "downtrodden".

WEEGEE: *(Pushing his hat further back on his head.)* Listen, Missy, you're gonna be in the paper. Most people are happy about that.

MERCY: You know what I'd be happy about? A trip to California, maybe.

WEEGEE: California's nothing but a pile of unemployed actresses covered by a thin layer of sand.

MERCY: For your information they have irrigation now. The trees are green, the ocean's blue, the people are so beautiful the whole state's like an aquarium full of tropical fish.

WEEGEE: Sure, if by fish you mean sharks.

MERCY: You know all about the big world.

WEEGEE: I know this is quite a building you got here. You get a murder almost every week.

MERCY: Well this is my first.

Beat.

MERCY: Tell me about eating in restaurants.

WEEGEE: It's like getting a hooker, but with food.

MERCY: They just bring you whatever you want?

WEEGEE: Well, sometimes you get more like a reasonable facsimile. If you don't like it, some places, you can send it back.

MERCY: Sounds like heaven.

WEEGEE: If circumstances were different, I'd take you.

MERCY: You would not.

WEEGEE: Sure I would.

MERCY: On a date?

WEEGEE: If you'd call it that.

MERCY: How would it go?

WEEGEE: What?

MERCY: Our date. Ask me. Just for practice.

WEEGEE: Uh… Things'll be a while here. You wanna go get some dinner?

MERCY: *(Coy.)* I don't know.

WEEGEE: It's rare I get a murder before suppertime. Your mother there just made me ten dollars. Provided that stain's spectacular enough to make the front page. What do you say?

MERCY: I don't know anything about you.

WEEGEE: I told you, I'm famous.

MERCY: And you want to have dinner with me?

WEEGEE: Sure.

MERCY: Why would you?

WEEGEE: Why wouldn't I?

MERCY: Maybe I'm grieving.

WEEGEE: You still gotta eat.

MERCY: I don't have anything to wear.

WEEGEE: You look dressed to me.

MERCY: Gee. *(To the COP.)* Sir! Hello! Officer! I need to go down the hallway, to the can. He'll come with me. As security.

COP: No.

MERCY: *(Squints at his cards.)* Are you cheating?

COP: What?

MERCY: You are! What's the point? You're playing against yourself!

COP: Go! Go to the goddamn can! But cherish it! Cherish every last moment of freedom you spend in that filthy crapper!

He makes his hanging gesture, then stares intently down at his cards, shutting her out.

MERCY: Okay Mr. Enchanté, take me away. Wait!

She reaches around on the floor underneath the sofa, finds a pen. She draws an arc of even circles up and around her collarbone.

They're my pearls. It's a childhood trick. It makes me feel glamorous. How do I look?

WEEGEE: Mildly eccentric.

He begins to take a picture. She puts her hand over the lens.

MERCY: Do you drive an automobile?

WEEGEE: I drive a Chevrolet.

MERCY: Ooh.

A beat. She steals charmingly from the room. WEEGEE follows.

COP: Read 'em and weep.

He lays down a card. Suddenly he realizes he's alone.

Shit.

He grabs his hat and tears out after them.

Black.

Scene 3

WEEGEE drives. MERCY sits beside him, up in her seat, exhilarated. They're in a convertible. The night city unrolls behind them in film noir. It's windy. WEEGEE tries to yank MERCY down so she sits lower in the car.

WEEGEE: Watch it!

MERCY: Why?

WEEGEE: Bridges. Wires. Whatnot.

MERCY: I'm short!

WEEGEE: You'll be shorter still when you're decapitated.

MERCY: Do you know what's better about real driving than movie driving? The whooshy sound. And the, well the way things are blurry. Is it always like this?

WEEGEE: What?

MERCY: Driving, so thrilling?

WEEGEE: At least hold onto something! *(She puts a hand on his head.)* Something solid! *(She moves it.)* So is there somewhere I can drop you? Maybe the library? You could go to work?

MERCY: I don't work at the library any more. After my mother lost her leg she wanted me close. When she gets, got, loaded she'd get the occasional sense she still had two legs and fall over. So I work the market on the block. To be accessible.

WEEGEE: Oh yeah? You like it?

MERCY: Sure, I know the prices of all the boxes. The cans too. It's fascinating.

WEEGEE: Why don't I drop you at the library anyway.

MERCY: Let's just drive around.

WEEGEE: I'm not a taxi service.

MERCY: I've seen you before, on the block. When that boxer got shot you took pictures of the kids watching.

WEEGEE: Yeah, well…I used to run a pony ride in your neighbourhood. Before your time. Pony pictures. You ever see that?

MERCY: No. Is it dirty?

WEEGEE: No! You rent a pony, walk it around. You take photographs of kids sitting on it. Slum kids go nuts for animals.

MERCY: Don't condescend.

WEEGEE: Hey I'm one myself. My brother and I shared a mattress you wouldn't bury a pig in. It's a great racket though, the pony ride. What mother doesn't want a picture of her tot sitting on top of a small horse?

MERCY: Hey, can I listen to the radio?

WEEGEE: Uh—

She's already turned it on. It plays quietly underneath.

MERCY: Which newspaper do you work for?

WEEGEE: I guess the one you'd call the communist one.

MERCY: Oh yeah? Do they pay you or do you just give them the pictures?

WEEGEE: Sit down!

MERCY: Can I drive?

WEEGEE: On second thought, keep standing. I'll just push you out when we pass the police station.

MERCY: *(Sitting.)* You wouldn't do that.

WEEGEE: Wouldn't I? Listen, it's fun to take a ride, it's cute for you to squirm around in my car, but that's all it is. So tell me where to drop you.

MERCY: At least give me a moment to think.

WEEGEE: Hey! My favourite song!

He turns up the radio, bouncing in his seat. He begins to sing along.

Down on the farm there's a picnic brewin'
Who's gonna be there?
All the aunts and cousins.
Out in the field there's hay needs a' mowin'
Who's gonna do it?
All the sons and brothers.
On the windowsill there's some pies a' coolin'
Who's gonna eat them?
Every mother's father.
Every day's a sunny day
Apple cheeks and fresh cut hay

To MERCY.

Hey, you know it!

MERCY: This is my favourite song too!

They sing together.

Over in Europe there's a war a brewin'
Who's gonna fight it?
All the boys and men.
Inside the factories revolution foments
Who's gonna quell it?
Send the police in.
In the cities downtown the poor are a'starvin'
Who's gonna feed them?
Not the government.

BOTH: Every day's a sunny day
Apple cheeks and fresh cut hay

Down in the basement water is rising
Who's gonna drain it?
Garble garble gen
Up in the kitchen the stove is burning
Who's gonna put it out?
Blah ba blah ba blah
In the middle of the ceiling a stain is spreading
Who's gonna bleach it?
Eh eh eh eh eh!

The stain is rising in the factory!
War is brewing in the basement farm!
The poor are eating fresh cut apple cheeks!
The fathers are mowing the boys and men!

Coy:

WEEGEE: Who's getting mowed?

MERCY: I like to get mowed!

WEEGEE: Who wants to get mowed?

MERCY: Oh please, please me!

BOTH: Every day's a sunny day!

Apple cheeks and fresh cut hay!

Song ends. Rabid hissing from behind. WEEGEE pulls a police radio from the back seat. He listens intently, decoding the crackly noise. It's like his whole body is salivating.

MERCY: What? What is it?

A voice from the radio says: "Five-Alarm Fire at Avenue A and Canal." The stage erupts into a five-alarm fire.

Scene 4

Tenement fire. Sirens, hoses, clamour. A MOTHER keeps tossing babies and animals out the window to a waiting FIREMAN. An OLD MAN stands traumatized. He looks like he's wearing every item of clothing he ever owned—sweaters, three pairs of pants, an overcoat…In his arms he clutches his one good suit, still on the hanger. MERCY watches, agog. WEEGEE has just taken a photo of the mother.

MERCY: Oh my God.

WEEGEE: Please. Don't appeal unless you believe.

MERCY: I was raised Catholic.

WEEGEE: But do you believe it?

MERCY: It's hard for some of it not to stick. Isn't there something…

WEEGEE: You can do? What? You gonna grow wings and save that lady? You gonna become a rain cloud and sprinkle us all with— Wait a…

WEEGEE takes a photo of the OLD MAN. The OLD MAN starts.

OLD MAN: *(Moaning.)* Ohh… Ohhh! You want my suit?

WEEGEE: Nah, nah.

MERCY: It'll be all right, sir.

OLD MAN begins to cry.

WEEGEE: Don't embarrass him with your pity. Or go ahead. Whatever you like!

MERCY: He's crying!

WEEGEE: And if he shit in the street would you wipe his ass with your hand? It's sad. So much is sad. What can you do? You're not a repository for all the sadness in the world.

He hands the OLD MAN his handkerchief, scouts for a new shot. MERCY follows him.

MERCY: I don't feel like I'm any kind of "repository." Just because a person feels something for the people around him doesn't mean they're a…

The woman throws a dog to the fireman.

Hey, do you ever feel strangely attracted by disaster?

WEEGEE: Only insofar as it's my business.

MERCY: Sometimes I sit around in the evenings imagining horrible things that could happen to me. I read a book where a girl is kidnapped and the thugs torture her by burning the soles of her feet with a clothes iron. Wouldn't that be terrible? God, it's so much hotter than you'd expect!

WEEGEE: It's fire.

MERCY: I know, I can't believe it! Just last night I was in my apartment, listening to the radio.

WEEGEE: Did you hear me? I do an advertisement. "Yellow Stripe Film, I endorse it!" But I don't recommend it.

MERCY: Ha ha. No, the President was on.

WEEGEE: Oh yeah? You think the possibility of war justifies us having to listen to that sanctimonious fathead talk?

MERCY: No, I—

WEEGEE: Did he stir you into a patriotic frenzy. Did you feel like unraveling all your antimacassars to crochet up a tank.

MERCY: Sure! I'm weepy and sentimental, I'm an idiot, I—

WEEGEE: I didn't say—

MERCY: You won't let me finish! I don't go out, I'm saying!

WEEGEE: I always go out!

The WOMAN throws a dog out the window to the FIREMAN. WEEGEE snaps.

MERCY: This is some dinner you've taken me to. Some barbeque!

The woman throws a cat to the FIREMAN, then the fire overcomes her and she begins to burn. MERCY looks away.

MERCY: Oh!

WEEGEE: I've got it. Let's go.

MERCY: Let's go?

WEEGEE: Come on!

They exit. The COP appears. He seems to sense they've been there. He does a dainty soft shoe, then exits on their trail.

Scene 5

The Opera. A crowd. MERCY stands behind WEEGEE. WEEGEE is pressed up at the edge of the red carpet. Someone has just gone in the door. WEEGEE is preoccupied, waiting.

MERCY: Is there a crime here?

WEEGEE: Nah I just like the opera. You ever been?

MERCY: Sure, when my yacht's in dock.

WEEGEE: I was with the cops last week, they confiscated a truckload of counterfeit alphabet books. Made in Korea, imported by the mob, destined for schools. Started with A is for ax, ended with Y is for yacht.

MERCY: Gee.

WEEGEE: You can imagine the damage to fragile minds.

MERCY: What are you looking for?

WEEGEE: A shot.

A OPERA PATRON—black tie, tails, cigar—appears.

WEEGEE: Mister!

He gets a good shot.

MERCY: You don't seem like the opera type.

WEEGEE: Hey there's cheap seats. You might like it too. A little culture.

MERCY: *(Dubious.)* I don't know. I saw a play once.

WEEGEE: Oh yeah, what?

MERCY: The Count of Monte Cristo.

WEEGEE: *(Snorts.)* That doesn't count!

MERCY: That's what I thought. I had an "uncle," he took my mother and me. The rest of the audience ate it up but I didn't find the count very convincing. His wig was made of yarn. I thought, this is "the theatre" people talk so much about.

WEEGEE: *(Watching down the carpet.)* You read too much. It's made you literal.

MERCY: No, I just I… Do I really want to see say, *Romeo and Juliet* with hair like an old sweater and a cardboard dagger? I see it just fine in my head.

WEEGEE: There's your problem.

A MATRON in a long white dress and tiara—the effect is very grandma-Halloween—has just exited a car and is tottering up the carpet.

MERCY: Look at that! Look at those diamonds! Are they real?

WEEGEE: Realer than she is. Go trip her.

MERCY: What?

WEEGEE: Go trip her. I want the picture.

MERCY: She's an old lady!

WEEGEE: Ah she's a vampire in a human body. You know where those diamonds come from?

MERCY: A cave in Africa?

WEEGEE: No, some shmo, your "uncle" let's say, licks dirt off the bottom of car tires in some automated factory, or some other shmo cuts up cow bellies in a slaughterhouse for fifty cents a year. Well that nice old lady owns that factory and that slaughterhouse and it's her money digesting up all those shmos until the life is sucked out of them and they're left with nothing and she's shitting diamonds. Go trip her for me!

MERCY: What did you mean, "there's your problem"?

WEEGEE: I mean, so you see something fine in your head. What's the point if that doesn't correlate to the reality of the larger world? Quick, go trip her! It'll be fun!

He pushes her out onto the carpet. MERCY looks around—she's kind of delighted by the sneakiness of it. Or maybe not. The MATRON holds her hand out to MERCY like to a stray dog.

MATRON: Don't be afwaid, dear.

She reaches into her evening purse.

MATRON: *(As though to an idiot child.)* Would'a wike a penny?

MERCY: Huh?

MATRON: *(Sings.)* Pwetty penny
Oh, pwetty money
Wike a penny?
Penny, honey?

Would'a wike a pwetty penny?
Spend it on a yummy candy?
Would'a wike a sparkwy penny?
Save it then you'w have some money?

Don't worry
I feew wesponsibwe
You poow thing
Wet me hewp you

The MATRON suddenly holds a giant penny above her head. The giant pennies multiply, somehow.

Would'a wike a wittwe jobee?
You won't be a swummy swobby!
Sitting in a hotew wobby
Pwostitutes awe vewy naughty!

MERCY: Prostitute!

MATRON: Come hewe deaw
Wet me save you
You poow thing
You don't know bettew
Have a penny, have a penny…

Enraged, MERCY grabs the MATRON's penny and clocks her. Laughing his head off, WEEGEE takes the picture. The radio crackles. WEEGEE's ears prick—something important. MERCY sees—just on the periphery—the COP. Maybe even just his leg, stepping into view from the knee down. She is frozen. He doesn't see her yet. The moment is broken and MERCY rushes off with WEEGEE.

They go. The COP enters. He sniffs. He looks up. He flips open his notebook.

COP: She was seen in a Chevrolet convertible. Hm. She was sighted "loitering" at a five-alarm fire. Did she start it?

(He sniffs the air.) She was here. Yes. *(Jots down.)* "Opera." If I were facing *(Does his hanging gesture.)* I think I'd see a movie. *(He lets out an operatic note, laughs.)* You can't hide forever, Little Mercy.

With surprising speed and stealth, he exits.

Scene 6

Murder scene. Very quiet. WEEGEE snaps away. MERCY lingers at the edges. Two BODIES—a man and a woman—lie dead. Handkerchiefs cover their bloody heads. A WITNESS twitches and flaps between the corpses. This is a song:

WITNESS: Can't a man walk around all night minding his own business without having people die in front of him! Well, can't he? There are more dead people than live people. In the world, statistically. As a boy I'd lie on the floor underneath the piano thinking of all the Indians buried underneath the house. And not just Indians. Where are the cops? Death haunts this world like a ghost. Everyone should die sooner, we live too long. We should live just long enough to feel like we're getting somewhere then POW POW! A trigger sparks an aneurysm. Everything's going to hell. The dead should consider themselves saved. They should consider themselves blessed. To be finished with all the shit. The fundamental betrayal of being alive. "You have so much potential." "Oh, you're mediocre." "We're willing you the house." "We sold it." "You're getting lucky tonight. You're beating your meat." "That stale éclair looked so delicious." Do you know what my family dies of? Insomnia. It's the opposite of insanity. You become so perfectly aware of everything you can't sleep. You can't sleep because you realize the treachery of relaxing. No one who understands the human condition can ever rest. The Book of Job is the Book of Life. Once you realize that it's like your whole body is made of witnessing eyes.

He collapses onto his knees. On either side of him, the BODIES rise. They do an awkward limb-askew dance. The WITNESS draws himself up, trembling, and joins them. WEEGEE does not see, but MERCY does. Sound of the COPS arriving. The BODIES fall dead again. The WITNESS looks around, terrified. WEEGEE grabs MERCY's hand, they exit.

Scene 7

The COP appears alone on stage. Maybe he dangles his baton in his hand. He's magnetic, playful, menacing, friendly, but mostly menacing.

COP: A dog likes a bone like
A bitch likes a slap
A dog guards his home like
A rat shuns the trap
A bone to a dog is a
Thorn in his back
The dog only moans when
His tight leash goes slack

Grrr…bark bark bark!

A dog likes to hunt like
A bitch likes to lie
A dog kills the runt like
A king shuts his eye
The hunt to a dog is the
Fruit in the pie
The dog never stops while
His prey is alive
Grrr… bark bark bark

He howls. His MINIONS enter.

A dog gets his bone as
a bitch gets her slap
The dog gets his bone 'cause
He's on her track
The dog keeps his home while
She quits the pack
Well I am that dog and
The bowl where I lap
Is

I'm telling you I'm telling you I'm telling

He's telling you he's telling you he's telling you.

I'm telling you I'm telling you I'm telling
You

Speaking, as though to MERCY.

Watch out.

Scene 8

Dark room. Everything red. WEEGEE is developing pictures, hanging them on a string to drip. MERCY watches, shielding her eyes. From where she sits, she can't see the photos.

MERCY: The newsroom really is just a room. I don't think I pictured it that way.

WEEGEE: Mghf.

MERCY: It doesn't seem to me like a newspaper could be generated just by people sitting at tables and chairs.

WEEGEE: There's a machine in the basement.

MERCY: *(Re: photos.)* Can I look?

WEEGEE: No.

MERCY: May I look?

WEEGEE: No.

MERCY: Is it the picture of me? You know that cup of coffee you bought me in the lobby doesn't count as dinner.

He ignores her. She sits in her chair, swinging her legs.

MERCY: I never seen a dead body before.

WEEGEE: No?

MERCY: Are you used to it?

WEEGEE: Sure. Nah. It's the children that get to you. They say that, but it's a true cliché. Earlier this week…a hit and run? Kid with a head like a deflated beach ball. Teeth trailing down the block. No joke, like Hansel and Gretel were gonna follow them to get to the face. It's funny, sure, later, but you think, this is a *kid,* a girl you could see, had maybe long eyelashes. She looked Italian, you know? Gold cross on her neck. A ginghamy dress. Then just, meat spilling out. Or, like the fire? I've seen a kid in a fire blacker'n the way they cook a fish down south. You may not believe it but I prefer to take pictures of the living. They've got more personality. Usually.

Beat.

MERCY: At the library, when I worked there, I was the only girl who ever read. Can you believe that?

WEEGEE: Knowledge isn't for everyone.

MERCY: Do you mean that everyone can't have it, or that everyone doesn't *want* it?

WEEGEE: What were you reading, "The Young Woman's Guide to Semantics"?

MERCY: No, novels!

WEEGEE: Oh, *novels.*

MERCY: I'm very partial to the French.

Beat.

WEEGEE: Isn't there someone who's…

MERCY: What?

WEEGEE: Responsible for you?

MERCY: Like a husband?

WEEGEE: Some kind of…minder. What about your father?

MERCY: What about him?

WEEGEE: Maybe you should go find him.

MERCY: You gonna lend me a shovel? I accept your condolences. But I never did see him. When he died, I mean. He was already gone. From the vicinity, not from the…

WEEGEE: Mortal coil?

MERCY: Yeah. Then he was just… more gone, I guess.
(Sings.) Brown sweater
that's what he called me
Come sit over here
that's what he told me
He was five-foot-five
I was maybe five years old
He was fixing an automobile
He wore a cardigan sweater
I think he was my father
I never felt better

He was a man I wanted to know
There for a second, where did he go?

MERCY talks to WEEGEE.

Why do they call jail "the big house"?

WEEGEE: I don't know. It's a big…house.

MERCY: Have you ever been?

WEEGEE: Not to stay.

MERCY: People eat rats in jail. They trade them for cigarettes like meat for money.

WEEGEE: Who told you that?

MERCY: I have ears! I don't live at a country club, you know! At the market, there are some boys who come around. They're in and out of jail. You should hear them talk.

WEEGEE: You could consider not believing them. It's a characteristic of the criminal classes that they're known to lie a little.

MERCY: I'm of the criminal classes.

WEEGEE: I'd say you're in a peculiar class of your own.

MERCY: Do you want to know how they eat the rats?

WEEGEE: No but you're going to tell me.

MERCY: They bail all the water out of their toilets, then they set a little fire and they roast the rats in the bowl.

WEEGEE: Ah, for…!

MERCY: *(Sings.)*
Little Morbid
that's what he called me
Try curling your hair
that's what he told me
He was the neighbourhood thug
I was in the neighbourhood of ten
He smoked Camel cigarettes
He gave me my first drag ever
I coughed and yet, and yet
I've seldom felt better

He was a man I wanted to know
There for a second, where did he go?

They hum. Then suddenly:

Maybe you have a picture of a steak over there somewhere?

WEEGEE: Hint again, I'm not a subtle man.

MERCY: You promised me dinner!

WEEGEE: I did not!

MERCY: Then promise it to me now!

WEEGEE: If you promise to shut up!

MERCY: That's not a very nice invitation!

WEEGEE: Shut up and I'll take you somewhere fantastic.

MERCY: Why am I skeptical?

WEEGEE: You're not shutting up!

MERCY: I will!

WEEGEE: Promise!

MERCY: I promise!
(Sings.)
Brown sweater
That's what he called me
Your hair is brown too
That's what he told me
I said "I can see that"
He said "You should know"
He was like a mountain of brownness there
In his cardigan sweater
We were brown together
I've never felt better

Her eyes slide over to WEEGEE, who develops, humming with her. She hums, eyes cocked sidelong at him, finishing with:

…all the men I wanted to know
Here for a second, then I don't know.

WEEGEE finds a half a candy bar stuck to a pile of photos. He hands it to MERCY. She takes a little bite.

Weegee, Mr. Weegee...I get such a warm feeling from you.

WEEGEE: Eat your candy bar.

A tiny beat.

MERCY: You know what? *(With arch delight.)* I betcha Hell looks a lot like this!

Scene 8 1/2

The COP holds a thin INFORMANT in a coat and hat up against the wall. We can't really see the INFORMANT's face. We don't have to.

COP: A thin girl, in a sweater and dress. Nondescript face. Catholic taste—likes fires, murder, and the works of Puccini. Her name is Mercy, Little Mercy, which is what she deserves and what she'll get! Have you seen her! Have you seen her! You're all the same, afraid to talk. I don't know where this fear of the police comes from. We're in an age that glorifies gangsters and corruption. What about the law! In small towns the police don't have to act like this! They don't have to lean on hopped-up runts to catch pint-size murderesses! No, in small towns, the cops lean on picket fences. They hold out their hands and bluebirds come perch on their fingers. Why? Because there the police consort with the lawful. They stand with the lawful against the phalanx of the bad. But here, you're all bad. I spend my days protecting people like you from people like you! Don't you think I'd rather be getting Johnnie's cat out of a tree!

INFORMANT: That's the fire department.

COP: *(Leans into the INFORMANT's throat, sings an operatic note or two.)* Little Mercy Callaghan, that's her name. You'll look for her. You'll be a fingernail on the long arm of the law.

Suddenly frees the INFORMANT.

Go! Go!

The INFORMANT scurries away.

COP: *(Waving his arms.)* I'm an octopus. I'm every animal that catches its prey, brings it to its mouth, and...

Takes a huge bite.

Black.

Scene 9

Sammy's Bar—a place for slumming. SAMMY cleans glasses behind the bar. NORMA DEVINE, a young and compelling drag queen, sits at the bar. She wears a kimono. They sing.

SAMMY:
Before things start
is the best time
when we wait in a pause
we can rest
Between events
we breathe slower
our hearts tucked away
in our chests

Every object appears
to be human
as it waits for its life
to begin
What will be used
lies unused, waiting
the pause makes those things
new again

NORMA:
The dressing room
is the best room

In make-up but not
in a dress
The drab of the day
is behind you
The glory of night still

BOTH: To come! What's to come is the best thing!
The future is never, not now!
What's to come is delight and perfection!
What's here is only here and now!

NORMA: I'm an eschata-
-logical woman
The apocalypse waits
In my head
I've a yearning
for something that's better
And yet still
I don't hope for the end

SAMMY: I'm a practical man
on the surface
but inside I believe
in the vast
cosmology of potential
This glass may be
only a glass, but

BOTH: To come! What's to come is the best thing!
The future is never, not now!
What's to come is delight and perfection!
What is here is only here and now!

SAMMY: Later there'll be midgets dancing
in the cabaret there on the stage
debutantes with their dates will be watching
the freaks and the whores on parade

NORMA: Later tonight I'll be singing
in the cabaret there on the stage
the joint will be packed SRO, kid
'cause Norma Devine's all the rage

BOTH: But now the lacuna of waiting
is the second before lovers kiss
the past and the future suspended
in the space between those lovers' lips
What's to come, what's to come is the best thing
The future is never, not now
What's to come is delight and perfection
What is here is only here and now

Sound of the door. NORMA exits. WEEGEE enters, MERCY trailing after. They take a table. At some point soon, the INFORMANT enters.

WEEGEE: What do you drink?

MERCY: I don't.

WEEGEE: Well you should. What do you want? You want me to pick something for you? Maybe you would like a lady-drink, a "pink fandango" or an egg-cream. Or maybe just a jar of paint thinner.

MERCY: Are you trying to cheer me up or humiliate me?

WEEGEE walks up to the bar.

SAMMY: Mr. Weegee.

WEEGEE: Mr. Sammy.

SAMMY pours WEEGEE a drink without asking.

The lady'll have a…

SAMMY: Coca-Cola?

WEEGEE: Yeah. Throw in a little…

SAMMY tops the Coke with liquor. WEEGEE fidgets.

Slow tonight?

SAMMY: The society crowd'll be in later. I'm happy enough for a little peace.

WEEGEE: I'm not a handsome man, am I Sammy? But I'm a genius, so it doesn't matter.

SAMMY: I don't know. What's handsome, right? It's impossible to dissect. Some women like a dark man, some a fair man. Donkeys like horses.

WEEGEE: You're a politic man, Sammy. Buy yourself a round.

SAMMY nods, pockets the dough. WEEGEE sits.

What?

MERCY: What is it?

WEEGEE: Coca-Cola.

She takes a tiny, suspicious sip.

MERCY: It's weird tasting.

WEEGEE: They wash the glasses with a funny soap.

He leans back in his chair, leans forward, takes off his hat, mushes his hair around, puts his hat back on. MERCY laps at her drink.

WEEGEE: I saw a man today fall out a—

MERCY: You told me that already!

WEEGEE: How's your drink?

MERCY: You know, *(Takes another little lapping sip.)* before today I only knew about death from books.

WEEGEE: Oh yeah like what?

He drains his glass, then waggles it in SAMMY's direction.

MERCY: Tolstoy.

WEEGEE: Tolstoy?

MERCY: He was a great writer!

WEEGEE: Forgive me my dear but death is not Anna Karenina throwing herself under a train.

MERCY: Why not.

WEEGEE: Because that's a dramatic gesture.

MERCY: She was unhappy! Her husband wouldn't divorce her. She thought her lover was unfaithful.

WEEGEE: She was a romantic heroine with dark eyes and a lot of hair and a bunch of dresses. Her death was not real—don't interrupt me!—because it was "meaningful" and death such as it is, is nothing.

MERCY: Oh it's something!

WEEGEE: It's nothing! A body without a person in it might as well be a duck hanging in a Chinese butcher's window. When that cop pulled the knife out of your mother did she scream? No, because she wasn't there.

SAMMY deposits a drink in front of WEEGEE.

Death is de facto the absence of life. Absence. *(To SAMMY.)* No, stay. Sammy's a smart man. Tell this little lady about death.

SAMMY: Whose death?

WEEGEE: Anyone's.

SAMMY: I don't like to generalize.

WEEGEE: Tell her about the guy in here died on his stool.

SAMMY: *(Smiles a little, remembering.)* Well, that gentleman just died.

WEEGEE: *(Prompting.)* And what made you notice it?

SAMMY: He never ordered another drink.

They chuckle.

WEEGEE: Bring me another, would you friend?

SAMMY goes.

WEEGEE: And a Coca-Cola for young Miss.

MERCY: I think you're condescending to me because you don't think I'm as worldly as you are.

WEEGEE: My dear lady you are not.

MERCY: I've had some experiences.

WEEGEE: Such as?

MERCY: My life. I couple that with what I've read and I think I've lived extraordinarily.

WEEGEE: *(Amused.)* Oh?

MERCY: Why is life only what you know of it? I can extrapolate outward. Do you know math? That's what they call it when you take the points that exist on a graph and, because of what you know happened, you can tell what will happen. Or what did happen.

WEEGEE: You mean you guess how things might go.

MERCY: No, I extrapolate. Take my mother,

WEEGEE: Please.

MERCY: Ah ha. Take my mother, she's a, was a, certain kind of humanity. I see her and what she does and I can, not guess, but know, I can know, how another person of a similar nature might react. Or feel. When she's, was, putting ice on her stump, do you think I don't know what a hundred other people all over the city are doing? Maybe not with a stump up on an orange knitted cushion, but—

SAMMY puts a new drink in front of her. She drinks from it not pausing.

MERCY: —mm, at the market I saw every kind of humanity. The kinds I didn't see I read about at the library. Every kind in between, I can extrapolate.

WEEGEE: Kid, that's making things up. People aren't math.

MERCY: Well they're not unknowable, either.

WEEGEE: I'm not saying they are. But you need to record the reality. You can't just go inventing it in your head.

MERCY: You invent! You're not God, you can't take a picture of everything at once.

NORMA enters in a tight-fitting red dress with exaggerated shoulders.

WEEGEE: I choose from *reality*.

MERCY: I'm just saying—

WEEGEE: I'm saying! I'm saying, live people are alive and dead people are dead and whatever you're talking about doesn't exist because it's not real.

MERCY: Maybe there's another life!

WEEGEE: Oh yeah? Harps and angels?

MERCY: Of the mind! What's in—

She jabs at her head.

WEEGEE: Devils and forks?

MERCY: You condescend.

WEEGEE: After life it's all a Catholic dress-up pageant, right? Like Norma over there in her…outfit.

NORMA daintily flips him off. MERCY is transfixed by her.

MERCY: Oh my.

WEEGEE: I'll tell you what you need, a more Judaistic concept of life. A focus on the here and now. You got a brain in your head, not *ether*.

NORMA drapes herself around WEEGEE.

MERCY: Is that your girlfriend?

WEEGEE: What? What?

NORMA: Am I? Darling, he doesn't know. He's confused.

SAMMY: Yeah his brain's all addled.

NORMA: It's all mixed up, isn't it. At the sight of me. You feel a little tippy. A little weak-kneed. A little collapsible?

She winks at MERCY.

WEEGEE: Norma, Mercy, Mercy, Norma.

NORMA: Am I interrupting something? *Romance?*

WEEGEE: Romance this.

MERCY: Are you an entertainer?

NORMA: I'm the entertainment.

MERCY: Will I get to see your act?

NORMA: Depends on how late you stay. When am I on, Sammy?

SAMMY: You're on last. You're always on last.

NORMA: The whole evening's built to build up to me.

SAMMY: It's true. Hey, you know how I remember who we got booked? I make a little rhyme of it.

(Sings.) Right at eight, the dwarf comes on
He does a dance to
L'Après-midi d'une faune
After him it's the chorus line of elderly ladies
Stripped to their underwear, each one over eighty
Then we got that fat broad who
Can't remember the words to her song but anyway
We keep her on, then it's the accordion guy who
Only talks through a puppet, he's shy, that's why

Anyone can be a star, in my bar

Then at ten when the swanky people
Arrive from uptown in their limousines
We got a pair of sisters whose animal impressions
All sound like chickens; they're followed by uh,
What's his name?, who recites a passage from
Dickens
In the voice of James Cagney who he claims once to
Have slept with, either that or they're brothers
Then some others, the pornographic balloon artist

ALL: Anyone can be a star in Sammy's Bar

SAMMY: At midnight we got that guy I bill as
The Blind Man's Fred Astaire; if you close your eyes
You can imagine him dancing there, but he's
Just standing there, he likes to stare, at the audience

SAMMY jumps up on the bar—the music tapdances; he does not.

ALL: Anyone can be a star in Sammy's Bar!

SAMMY: Then we got the wall-eyed man who'll
Eat any object the audience hands him
And then the skinny hoodlum who screams at
Patrons to give him their money, which I think is
funny

ALL: Anyone can be a star in Sammy's Bar!

SAMMY: Fifteen acts an evening, each one positioned—

ALL: Anyone can be a star!

SAMMY: Between the nadir and the apex of what—

ALL: Anyone can be a star!

SAMMY: You might consider entertainment, it's strange but—

ALL: Anyone can be a star!

SAMMY: Once it's on stage, and the audience pays, it's art!

ALL: Anyone can be a star…

SAMMY: …in Sammy's bar.

Song ends.

SAMMY: Nah! I lied. The only real star we have here is the beautiful, the irreplaceable…Norma Devine!

NORMA: Then I come on.

MERCY: And what do you do?

NORMA: What do I *do*?

MERCY: Yeah. Do you sing, or, or…?

NORMA: Do I sing. Do I sing, or or. You've picked yourself up quite a fluffy piece of lint, Mr. Weegee. But maybe that's what you like. A real woman would frighten you. Or maybe she's more Sammy's type. Why don't you take her into the stock room, Sammy, and show her a few unspeakable things.

SAMMY: I'm not like that! You of all people should know I'm not—

NORMA: Sure you are!

SAMMY: Don't make me think of hitting you!

MERCY: Don't talk to the lady like that! It's not nice!

NORMA: It's fine. Sammy just likes to make me quake.

SAMMY: You bait me. *(To MERCY.)* I'm a gentleman.

NORMA: Use those big strong arms to mix me a cocktail.

SAMMY makes NORMA a drink.

NORMA: A highball. In the town where I grew up, Mercy—

WEEGEE: *Little* Mercy.

NORMA: Little Mercy, in the town where I grew up you couldn't get a highball. A beer. A glass of wine. You couldn't buy a red dress. If you wanted to dance you had to wait 'til the corn was high so you had somewhere to hide.

SAMMY hands her a drink. She hands it back.

Go on, lover—bore yourself by mixing me a better drink. Where I'm from, if you didn't drop your Gs people thought you were a Bolshevik. A friend of my father's was run out of town because he was suspected of unionizin' his cows. No doo-doo. *(Smiles at MERCY.)* I was like you. A drab little mouse. Hiding away in my house. But I educated myself. Do you know about physics, Little Mercy?

WEEGEE: She knows about everything. Get her to explain math to you.

NORMA: Have you heard of the bomb they're working on? Everyone: Mussolini, Hitler, Hirohito, us? A bomb to rent the fabric of everything. Imagine the fabric of the universe torn in pieces so tiny they flew apart and became a poison. That's the direction the world is headed in.

MERCY: Really?

NORMA: *(Nods.)* It's why the great physicist Albert Einstein never wears socks. They're an insulator against the common flow of electrons. Hosiery is *divisive.* It leads us to believe we're separate from each other. So I just paint a line up the back of my leg.

WEEGEE: Because she's cheap.

NORMA: Because I want to be connected! We're all made out of the same particles! I can't even cut notches in my headboard any more; I feel too much empathy for the wood. *(Smiles at WEEGEE.)* Mr. Weegee, Mr. Weegee. So little confounds him, I think he must like it. Mercy's a nice name. You're lucky you were born with such a pretty name.

MERCY: I think you're an extremely pretty girl.

NORMA: Thank you. You don't have to dress like that, you know... Learn to sew. I make all my own gowns. My mother made sure...all her daughters learned to sew. Physics, sewing, the high, the low. A girl can't know too much, Little Mercy.

MERCY: I'd really like to see your number. I mean, now. I may not be here later.

NORMA: *(Thinks for a second.)* All right. *(To WEEGEE.)* Unlike some people I hate to disappoint a lady. Maestro!

She cocks her fingers like a gun at WEEGEE.

This is for you, you sex pistol.

(Sings.) Hidden deep in the Amazon
there's a prehistoric veldt
paleolithic and phantasmagorical
it lies inside the steaming void
left by a dead volcano
vines and trees and creepers grow there
covering a teeming temple

where bird-men and lizard-girls
and snake-boys and rhino-women
tiger-girls and werewolf-men
and chupalupa-acaluca-nuka-nuka-witcha-hexa
Love to do the rhumba-rhumba
Rhumba!
Rhumba!
Rhumba!

MERCY: Oh my God!

WEEGEE: What?

MERCY: I have to dance!

MERCY gets up and begins dancing. It's in the vein of what NORMA's doing, but obviously of MERCY's own housebound invention.

NORMA: You dance much, honey?

MERCY: No!

They really get a thing going. Then:

NORMA: Hidden deep in the Amazon
there's a prehistoric veldt
paleolithic and phantasmagorical
where cobra-men and python-women

MERCY: fruit-fly-girls and termite-ladies

NORMA: croco-dames and alligate-boys

MERCY: bloodsucking-boys and hairy werewolf men

NORMA: the worms that crawl up through your pee-pee
and eat out your brain!

MERCY: piranhas who pretend they're doctors!

NORMA: turtles who pretend they're doorknobs!

MERCY: man-boy, snake-boy, fish-boy, bat-boy

NORMA: rat-girl, cat-girl, thin-girl, fat-girl
And copulate like:

BOTH: nuka-nuka-witcha-hexa
Love to do the rhumba-rhumba

NORMA: Love to do the rhumba
Rhumba!

SAMMY stands on a chair, clapping and whistling.

WEEGEE: Siddown!

SAMMY: A round! A round for the beautiful Norma Devine!

NORMA: I'll drink to that!

MERCY: You're not a real woman, are you?

NORMA: Don't be a little bitch.

SAMMY hands her a shot. She tastes it.

MERCY: Sit with us. Sit with us, please.

NORMA: *(Shakes her head.)* I have to go change. There's this debutante comes in here, an Astor or…some scion of the inbred hotel gentry. "Astor." "Ass-tor." I'm the one with the ass-tornado! She's got nothing. A jalopy, a dust-bowl. Going to pick fruit for some bastard rapist California fruit grower, that's all her ass is good for! *(She downs her shot, licks her lips.)* When I stand next to the Ass-tor, she's gonna look like a carp in a sack!

NORMA tosses SAMMY her glass as she leaves. He catches it.

SAMMY: I'm in love with that woman.

MERCY: She's not really a—

SAMMY: You see how she doesn't even acknowledge me?

MERCY: But she does!

SAMMY: No. No. I bought her flowers and she told me they were "too blue." What the Hell! I took them back. They were too pink. Too red. Too yellow. What other colours are there? So now, no flowers. I give her a ten dollar bill and she buys them herself. I've read philosophy I understood better. *(To MERCY.)* You don't know! Women come to me! They knock on my windows at night. I have to throw rocks at 'em so they'll leave! *(To WEEGEE.)* Jesus. I go to the store and help her pick out fabric for her dresses. You should see that woman with her face pressed up against a roll of sequins. Each sequin was like a little picture of her face. I thought I'd die. Up against an army of Normas! I'm only one man!

WEEGEE: Hey, Sammy…

SAMMY: She uses me. If I made her clear her tab I could buy this block. *(Beat.)* She's a cockteasing whore. Sometimes I think I should kill her.

WEEGEE: Ah, don't talk shit. What would it solve?

SAMMY: Nothing. I want to stop loving her but it eats me up! I shave my beard, I grow a mustache, I wear a clean shirt, a dirty shirt…I bought a new hat. Nothing! She wants an intellectual man.

MERCY: You could read more.

SAMMY: If I did that she'd want a brute! I wish she was French.

MERCY: Why?

SAMMY & WEEGEE: French women are obvious.

SAMMY: Well they are! All they want is a smoke and a smack in the ass.

MERCY: Don't you think that's horribly reductive?

SAMMY: You been to France?

MERCY: I read *Madame Bovary.*

SAMMY: I lived there for two years shepherding a little flock of whores. Let me tell you those *demoiselles* were plenty *simple. Simple et sympathique.*

MERCY: Did it ever occur to you that you just thought so because you couldn't understand them?

SAMMY: I understood them plenty.

(Sings.) Dans les rue de Paris, les demoiselles flânent
avec leurs baguettes et leurs culottes sales
est-ce-qu'elles sont des putains, on ne sait jamais
les petits pieds parfaits, et les dents qui leurs fait mals

Dans les rue de Montmartre, elles se promenent
dans leurs fishnets et leurs talons hautes
est-ce-qu'elles sont des putains, on ne sait jamais
elles piquent le nez avec les ongles tellement longues

MERCY: I don't speak French.

WEEGEE & SAMMY: Si seulement tous les femmes étaient putains
une transaction simple, puis c'est fin
Pas de larmes, pas d'alarme, passe le pain
Si seulement tous les femmes étaient putains

MERCY: I don't understand a word! This is rude!

WEEGEE: You don't want to know.

MERCY: I want to know everything!

WEEGEE: In the streets of Paris, the young women loiter
with their long sticks of bread and their dirty
underwear
are they all whores, who can ever know
with their tiny perfect feet, and their bad hurting teeth

In the streets of Montmartre they walk around
in their fishnets and their high heel shoes
are they all whores, who can ever know?
they love to pick their noses with such long
fingernails

WEEGEE & SAMMY: If only all women were whores
A simple transaction, then it's done
No tears, no scenes, pass the bread
If only all women were—

MERCY throws her drink in WEEGEE's face.

MERCY: You make me sick.

WEEGEE: What about him?

MERCY: I don't know him well enough. *(She looks around as though coming to.)*

You make me so sick I could vomit. If I'd known you were like this I would never have…

She is not well.

SAMMY: Bathroom that way.

MERCY exits. WEEGEE mops his face with his shirt-tails. Sometime shortly, the INFORMANT exits.

So who's your little ladyfriend.

WEEGEE: She's just a girl.

SAMMY: You seem to like her.

WEEGEE: Do I?

NORMA: *(Off.)* Sammy!

SAMMY: Sir, I'm so deeply in love I can feel every vein in my heart.

WEEGEE: If thine eye offend thee, pluck it out.

SAMMY: Find me the surgeon who cut your heart out. That's what I say! Find him and goddamnit I'll give him every cent I have.

NORMA: *(Off.)* Sammy! Come zip me.

SAMMY grabs his crotch.

SAMMY: The tug of the leash, my friend.

He exits. WEEGEE is alone.

WEEGEE: "Cut my heart out."

Long silence. He sings.

On the beach at Coney Island, the faces of the people
People from the shtetl, people from Shanghai
families eating noodles, while underneath that
  blanket
a sailor tries to screw his date, the blonde with the
  curls
and old men with old-man breasts ogling the girls

In rooms, on grates, on fire escapes,
people spooned up with each other, dreaming
  better lives
then: bagels on a looping string, coffee in a thick cup
even when you wake up
there are good things in this world

An embarrassment of riches
If you could only see it, the way that I see it
You'd see…

Somewhere in a cinema, a teenage couple kissing
While a lady—she's got two teeth left—shakes and
weeps
and the plain girl on the balcony leans towards the
screen

Transformed by the movie from a
schoolgirl to a queen

(He talks.) You know what's great? The egomania, my friends, that's what's great. Everyone else, what's their continuity? God? Country? What's that when you're lying in your bed alone at night? What do you got? You got nothing. Pray to your God, but where the hell is he? *(Jabs at his head.)* In here. I used to play the violin. Sure I did! What, a man can't be good at two things? I fiddled at the movie theatres, back in the silent days? Make them scared of the villain, laugh at the jokes, cry at the romance 'til their eyes bled. Maybe it's cold. But I got love. For the subject. For the audience. I got love for you. *(Smiles a little sadly.)* But it ain't that kind of love. Or maybe it is, who knows. *(Manhandles his camera.)* I kiss this fuckin' machine every night like a wife. Photography, it's a great racket—there's nothing in the world to do but see!

(Sings.)

An embarrassment of riches, if you could only see it
In streets, in bars, in cop cars, people caught in
aftermaths of murders, or sooty from a fire
But those faces, cut and bruised, open up like
flowers
In our worst and finest hours
We let ourselves be seen

An embarrassment of riches, if you could only see it
the way that I see it, you'd see…

MERCY enters. Song ends.

How you feeling?

MERCY: Better. We should've eaten.

WEEGEE: I'll get you an olive.

MERCY: What time is it?

WEEGEE: Why, you gotta be somewhere?

MERCY: I'm worried about my mother. She can't be alone.

WEEGEE: She's dead; she's alone forever.

MERCY: I know, but... What will they do with her?

WEEGEE: Well, my guess is they'll give her an autopsy.

MERCY: There, on the bed?

WEEGEE: No, they'll roll her onto a stretcher and carry her down the stairs, put her in the back of a van. Then the coroner will saw through her ribs, crack her open. See what killed her.

MERCY: Why are you so unkind?

WEEGEE: You asked.

Beat.

MERCY: I get angry sometimes that I ever worked at that library. Not just the books but the size of the rooms... I think it's wrong to show people what they can't have. It's infuriating to be in a position to suppress your desires. *(Takes his hand.)*

WEEGEE: *(Pulls his hand away.)* You're in shock. You feel bad, it's normal.

MERCY: She wasn't so bad. I'm telling you. She was bad, but she wasn't so bad. What was your mother like?

WEEGEE: A Russian Jew so tiny you could stuff an egg with her.

MERCY: Big Mercy was an Irish Catholic so big she drank her husband under the table then out the door. I'm serious. A bottle a night, and that's when she was on the wagon. My father was small, like me. When

I was a baby my mother told me he was a leprechaun. Then she told me I was a changeling, not even hers really, but she kept me because who else would. Then when her leg came off she told me I was the leg's ugly twin. She'd try to grab me and stick me underneath her stump. I'm not making this up, she was crazy. She said she wouldn't vote because they wanted you to. She kept a Marxist pamphlet between her mattresses.

WEEGEE: Nothing wrong with Marx.

MERCY: She said the pamphlet was their wedding announcement.

WEEGEE: She couldn't read?

MERCY: Of course she could read. She was smart. It just... It pained her to know she was unimportant.

WEEGEE: Well, salut. *(He drinks.)*

MERCY: I'm sorry I threw the drink. I think I always wanted to do that. You don't really feel that way, do you?

WEEGEE: What way?

MERCY: About women. Because it's not right. Why would you want things to be less complicated?

WEEGEE: Because it's easier.

MERCY: Do you wish I was a whore?

WEEGEE: What kind of question is that?

MERCY: Well do you?

WEEGEE: I don't think you'd be suited to the lifestyle, no.

MERCY: Because you don't find me beautiful?

WEEGEE: I find you...I find you fine. Another soda?

MERCY: I'm a virgin.

WEEGEE: Ah, don't—

MERCY: A thirty-one-year-old spinster virgin. But I think about it. I spend all day giving people change. Touching their fingers. It's nice. Fifty cents, thirty cents…

He goes behind the bar.

What's your real name?

WEEGEE: I forget.

MERCY: No you don't.

WEEGEE: What does it matter?

MERCY: You know my name.

He measures out a big drink.

What does your wife call you?

WEEGEE: I don't have a wife.

MERCY: What does your girlfriend call you?

WEEGEE: Now you're fishing.

MERCY: What do your lady friends call you?

WEEGEE: A bastard. Then a cab.

MERCY: You're so glib.

WEEGEE: I don't like to worry.

MERCY: What if somebody worried about you?

WEEGEE: Then I'd worry about that. Have another Coke.

MERCY: You spiked it.

WEEGEE: Then have that olive I offered you.

MERCY: Don't you feel we have a kindred… something?

WEEGEE: What does it matter? Huh? Whether you like me or I like you. Ask Norma. Scientists have worked it out. It's just molecules, vibrating at different frequencies. Like the radio, the waves are just out there. So you catch them for a while. There's nothing permanent in human relations, Little Mercy.

MERCY: That's not true. You can't believe that. I like you.

WEEGEE: It's in your head.

MERCY: I liked you at once I saw you. The way you skulked around the room. I felt you understood the world in a different way. Like me.

WEEGEE: Well I don't. I see and I, occasionally I interpret. I don't understand it, though. I wouldn't want to. It would be like looking into the face of God, you'd go… *(He makes a hand-in-front-of-face/blind gesture.)*

MERCY: What's so hard about it. People want love. That's all. That's all I want.

WEEGEE: You'd do better to want a million dollars. Sammy and Norma there? That's love. Even the war is a horrible, misplaced love. Love is just a need that can go awry. When you feel it, either turn it into something you can control, or cut it out. Cut it out and replace it with…

MERCY: What?

Little beat.

You have love. For other people? I saw it when you gave that man your handkerchief. When you said you'd buy me dinner. When you gave me that little piece of candy bar.

WEEGEE: I have…a measure of compassion.

MERCY: Is that all?

WEEGEE: Yes.

MERCY: Are you sure?

He is not.

You should think about it because…I don't think people get so many chances.

Beat.

Well. This is the most exciting place I've ever been. Will there really be debutantes later?

WEEGEE: And gangsters and molls and dwarves dressed as clowns and anything else you might want.

MERCY: Talking dogs?

WEEGEE: Probably.

MERCY: This is me, being charming.

WEEGEE: You're very.

SAMMY and NORMA enter. NORMA wears a foxy silver number that in better light might look trashy but in this light looks elegant. It's still unzipped.

NORMA: Cop a feel like that again and I'll snap your arm off!

SAMMY: The zipper's stuck!

NORMA: I'll break it like a twig. You! Mercy! Come help Norma.

SAMMY throws up his hands, goes behind the bar, sulking. MERCY fiddles with the zipper.

Ask a man to zip your dress and he molests you! I should wear armour, like Joan of Arc!

MERCY struggles with the zipper. NORMA grunts and fidgets. SAMMY is far away.

MERCY: I don't understand. Don't you like him?

NORMA: More than you can imagine.

MERCY: Then why won't you let him touch you? Wouldn't you like him to…

NORMA: Just shut up.

MERCY: He's in love with you. I heard him say it.

NORMA: My magic doesn't bear close scrutiny, Little Mercy. Think about it.

MERCY: Oh.

NORMA: Yeah. What's the holdup?!

MERCY: It's really stuck.

NORMA: Sammy, hand me a corkscrew!

SAMMY: *(He does.)* Knock yourself out.

NORMA fiddles; no dice.

NORMA: Okay, help me. But keep a leash on those weasily mitts.

SAMMY: You made the dress! If it doesn't work—

NORMA: A leash! And I'll let you draw my stockings after.

SAMMY grunts something that sounds like "cocktease." NORMA grunts something that sounds like "jerk." NORMA turns on the radio.

MERCY: *(To WEEGEE.)* Hey, will you dance with me?

WEEGEE: I don't—

MERCY: Please.

WEEGEE considers. He and MERCY come together with false tries. SAMMY has got

NORMA's zipper up. She sits on the bar with a bent leg and he carefully draws a line up her calf.

MERCY: I feel like Nora Charles in *The Thin Man*.

WEEGEE: Don't mock my girth.

MERCY: They're a detective couple. He, Nick, the Thin Man, is tall and very smart; he's an alcoholic but you don't mind it. She, Nora, is petite and very *soignée;* she wisecracks and smokes, but he loves her. Their apartment is huge. It's in a hotel and anytime they want something, they just ring. A man brings it up. The Thin Man mixes cocktails in the afternoon for everyone. Even the murder suspect.

WEEGEE: You've got it wrong. Nick Charles isn't the Thin Man.

MERCY: Shh! He wears a dressing gown. She wears a peignoir. He says things like, they're in a bar and he orders two martinis and she assumes he's ordered for her but then he says "What are you going to have?" She's not angry though because it's a joke between them. He would die for her, she knows it. But it's unsaid. They snap at each other, but the rest is unsaid, they're so in love.

WEEGEE and MERCY are very light on their feet.

NORMA: The stars are all out tonight
You'd go blind if you tried to count them
The sky is lit up so bright
We cast shadows onto the fountain

There water flows from a cherub's eyes
into a cracked limestone basin
Is it wrong that I wish to go blind?
When all I see is not mine for the taking

Every star in the sky has already died
blackened and shrunk to a dead nub
The myth is that fire hides inside
But it's coal as cold as a dead shrub

So is the heat that we feel all a lie?
I burn outward and in, I'm a furnace
Is it wrong that I wish now to die?
Before your heat and my heat consume us
Consume us

SAMMY & NORMA: Go tie yourself to the tracks, my friend
No, your one-handed knots are untying
The train is gone anyway; it's not coming back
You try, but you cannot die trying

ALL Every star in the sky has already died
Blackened and shrunk to a dead nub
The myth is that fire hides inside
But it's coal as cold as a dead shrub

So is the heat that I feel all a lie?
I burn outward and in, I'm a furnace
Is it wrong that I wish now to die?
Before your heat and my heat consume us…
Consume us…

The door slams, ending the song prematurely. A PAPERBOY enters.

PAPERBOY: Extra extra read all about it! Woman murdered in tenement stabbing! Grisly murder shocks police! Full-page photo by Weegee the Famous, crime picture genius! Grisly murder, read all about it! Tenement stabbing shocks police!

The door slams again. The COP enters.

COP: I'll take a paper.

The PAPERBOY enters. The COP pats him on the head, winks.

Pay you later.

He opens the paper. On the front page is a picture of MERCY standing over her mother's body.

"Little Mercy Callaghan, librarian, stands over the body of her mother, Mercy Callaghan, a laundress." It's quite a picture. The light. The shadow. The cinema. No mention of me. I'm sure that's an oversight. As Miss Callaghan here is, of course, our star.

MERCY looks around. Nobody else seems real. A strangely rousing reprise.

ALL: I wouldn't eat a cookie
to remind me of my life
I'd rather eat that knife
A hundred knives and razor blades
Would taste to me like lemonade
But the taste of my past

Proust says a madeleine
What about a woman then?
Freud says that every man
What about a woman then?
What about a woman then?
What about a woman then?
What about a woman then?
What about a woman then?

MERCY: *(Over them.)*
I've never had a madeleine…
I've never had a madeleine
I've never had a madeleine
I've never had a madeleine!

(Talks.) Maybe somebody would be good enough to write this down. *(Nobody does.)* I, Little Mercy Callaghan, confess. I confess that in that room, that tiny room with that…inconceivably large woman, I felt sometimes that the walls would melt if I

couldn't shut myself off. Where do you go, with energy like that? My mother didn't know. That hairy bathrobe she wore had worn her so penitent she'd bled out any… *(Holds her fingers spread like, "heft.")* But I remember her in a dress and the people who would come round, just to hear her talk. Men. Ladies. She was a dynamo in the pure sense, an engine of energy. But all the things in the world, they'll take that from you. In dribs and drabs, they suck it out. Big Mercy had a heyday of about three years. Probably. Maybe. *(Beat.)* I went to the country once. With an "uncle." We swam in a lake and there were leeches. I didn't catch any, I mean, sucked to me, but I saw one, out of water, cross a rock. A leech cross a dry rock. Out of its environment, can't breathe, can't see, does a leech even have a mind?, but crossing a rock, sensing the water and moving towards it. And I let it, I didn't crush it. It wants to be in the water. That's where it belongs. But what if there is no water? What if the leech is searching and there's no place to go? In her last days my mother lay on that couch watching the new gangrene meander its way up her side. Her eyes were like two leeches, trying to crawl out of her head. Just to get away. From the gangrene. From her life. I couldn't stand it any more! There was no water for my mother, ever. She thought there was. But I knew all along! *(Beat.)* I'm a floor cleaner and a cash-out girl! I sell you a pack of cigarettes! But I could, I could, Oh! I could tell you about foreign policy. I could talk appeasement, I could talk gold standard, I could talk Tolstoy, I could imagine architecture, I could tell you why the cities are crumbling as they grow. I could explain to you why dissonance in music is necessary. I could tell you why passion redirects itself into art. Heaven. Hell. Breughel, Dostoevsky, I KNOW IT! The thoughts in my head are so…packed! So packed in when you, when you cut up my head to see why I'm so bad the pressure should... *(Realizing the absurdity, but saying it.)* the room will be covered in brains!

The COP moves suddenly, swifly—he pins her up against the bar with her hands behind her back, gets out his cuffs. She tries to twist away, animal-like.

MERCY: Oh God! Don't make me go! It's so good here! It's so good!

WEEGEE: Mercy!

MERCY: Yes! YES!

MERCY turns around, hopeful. A flash. The moment is for a second frozen as WEEGEE takes her picture.

Scene 10

Almost like the first scene. WEEGEE stands with his camera. MERCY sits alone also, this time in the back of a paddy wagon. Her hands are handcuffed in front of her.

WEEGEE: Ten dollars, one murder. Twenty-five dollars, two murders. Twelve for a fire. Jack for the opera, maybe three-five bucks.

(Beat.) It's a fifty dollar night. I should celebrate. Get a bottle, get a whore, go to town. *(Beat.)* You know I never got more tail than when I ran that pony ride. Can you believe that? I didn't ask mostly, they threw themselves at me. Every mother wants a picture of her tot on a horse. You know what got 'em, I mean for the picture not the hm-hm? It wasn't the horsie. It was the little song I sang. Just a ditty. *(Sings.)* Don't you want a pony ride?/Step up for a pony ride/two dollars for a child/three dollars for a *(High note.) pair...*

He squints upward like a choirboy, clears his throat. Attempting to perfect the reedy note.

Pair…

The note hangs in the air as WEEGEE disappears.

MERCY: Dress up
in a dress
Put on
some high heels
Then wear
a straw hat
Step out
in the street
The bus
takes four days
to get to
the sea
When you
arrive at
the sea

It's raining
It's raining

When your
straw hat is full
Take it
down to the sea
With the
rain on your head
And the
salt on the beach
Set your
hat in the sea
Step your
feet into the sea
Walk your
legs into the sea

Duck your
head underneath the sea

The ocean is calm when it's black
The water turns blue and then warm
White fish swarm as pale as a wreck

There's no storm
There's no storm
There's no storm

MERCY looks around, her hands are calm in her lap. A police radio crackles, off.

Black.

The End